I0429410

Chapter 1

The real underlying problem is a seeming contradiction about the experience of "rights in Mankind":
1. Found to "be there"

vs.

2. Created to "be there"

Clearly, experience of "rights in Mankind" is not questioned. And by an attempt to declare:

Mankind has no rights "within".

A potential unanimous response by all of Mankind, by resounding declaration would be:

Mankind clearly has rights "within".

Clearly "rights within Mankind exist and are experienced".

Are the "rights within Mankind":
1. Found by Mankind. "There before experienced."

OR

2. Created by Mankind. "Created before experienced."

If Mankind has the tiniest amount of responsibility to BE THE CAUSE of "rights within Mankind", then possibility exists for Mankind to be saved "from Mankind". Why? Because, if "rights within" can only possibly be FOUND, then Mankind is subject to FIND "rights within" for potentially every living thing on Earth (possibly every non-living thing as well).

Chapter 2

The concept, model or idea for "rights within" must have an origin.

A right to continued life, to continue living life is a "right within" for every individual person alive today on Earth.

Did this "right within" originate by self? Was "self" the first person to declare this "right within" for self? Or was this claim, this declaration of "right within" to continue life, to have life, to live among Mankind, to survive, a declaration/claim by another prior to "self"?

Before "self", that claim/declaration was by "family". Parents did this!

How could this have any importance with respect to "rights within"? Well...before "self" could speak or gesture or contained capacity to make this claim/declaration to have this "right to survival within", the family did make this claim/declaration on behalf of "self" ("self" as a child). This fundamental "right within" originated in "family". Family is the source of this specific "right within".

What are the steps? How did "family" create this "right within"?

Chapter 3

The family model begins with two prospective spouses.

Preparation for a child is most usual.

Enter "the child" and suddenly "new roles" exist somehow.

The family model may provide the clearest description for how "new roles" come into existence. First, any attempt to describe "parent role" does not exist and is not experienced needs the attempt to cease. Obviously, "the child" role and "the parent role" does exist and is experienced.

Did "the child" create or cause "the parent"? Did "the parent" create or cause "the child"?

The more appropriate question is:
Did spouse have any decision, claim or declaration "requirement" to suddenly "become parent"?

Clearly, a spouse can completely ignore "the child". Such behavior has many descriptions which all converge into various forms of not-human or irresponsible. This is possible by a potential father and even a birthing mother. These behaviors may have excuse or exception, but these behaviors are very very rare, and allowed excuse in those rare events is possible, but only remotely possible.

The spouse, by most frequent "opposite response to ignore", must ACT. What ACT is this? The ACT is by sovereign declaration:
"I am a parent to this child from now on."
"This child will call me parent/father/mother."
"I will call this child mine, my responsibility."
"I will provide for this child."
"I will seek the needs of the child and seek to satisfy those needs."
"I will embrace complaint from this child."

These declarations create!

Here is the key to the family model.

Chapter 4

In the book "The Invisible Person: I" chapter 3, "created my own experience" of connection begins the chapter. If "created" is the incorrect description, the only remaining possibility for the connection experience described is "found". Are two persons only capable of "found", having no possible contribution for causing a shared connection experience?

"Found" has mystery and excitement as though hunting for treasure has produced treasure at long last. But "found" removes all responsibility completely.
"Created" may feel lacking mystery and excitement though.

For beginning relationships, for dating, for prospective spouses and actual spouses, it may be best to allow both "found" and "created" possibilities.

But the declaration by parent did create!

Here is the key to the family model.

By declaration, by sovereignty more clear to be sovereign than any nation, a declaration is an act by the invisible person (TIP) described in these books:
> "The Invisible Person"
> "The Invisible Person: I"
> "The Visible Person: I"

By sovereign declaration, the "role of father" is created and the "rules for role of father" is created.

Any attempt to say "role of father does not exist" will be met with harsh debate, perhaps a violent response. The attempt to deny existence of "role of father" is not about a "role" or "group" or "category". The attempt to deny existence of "role of father" is about experience of existence of "role of father".

The attempt to deny experience is very often met with violent response (as is attempt to accuse experience "not experienced").

What father would allow "role of father" is not experienced? What mother would allow "role of mother" is not experienced? What parent would allow "role of child" is not experienced by the child?

The most important point is "experience". But "experience" always has a target, an "aimed at" (AA) for what is experienced. And the only possibility for "what is experienced" is "role of father" (mother, parent, etc.).

For the family model, declaration literally creates existence of "role of father" and the existence of "role of father" is literally experienced by father. That father creates "role of father" and then "enters into role of father" and experiences all aspects of life "through role of father". The only description which matches is "perspective". The "role of father" is a created perspective by sovereign declaration within.

In the book "The Invisible Person"(TIP), it is TIP that makes declaration, experiences experience, observes observation and more. In the book "The Visible Person: I", TIP is described in "book description/overview" through real life description of "before a mirror". TIP creates perspective which enables all of life to be "experienced through" completely. Any attempt to deny perspective exists and is experienced is exactly the same attempt to deny "role of father" exists and is experienced.

Summary:
"Role of father" exists and is experienced.

Chapter 5

AFTER "role of father" is created by declaration and is experienced, the experience of "role of father" is immediately followed by connection experience with "role of father".

Again, attempt to deny connection exists between TIP and "role of father" is also an attempt to deny experience of connection.

Connection is experienced and therefore exists.

AFTER "rules for role of father" are created by declaration and experienced, the experience of "rules for role of father" is immediately followed by connection experience with "rules for role of father".

Deny the connection to test whether the connection exists or just accept connection is experienced and therefore exists.

"Within" the "role of father" perspective, the connection as father with child is experienced.

Father declares "father" to child and teaches child to declare "son" to father.

These are the bonds in the family model. These are the connections experienced in the family model. The "roles" are experienced. Both connections and "roles" are experienced and therefore do exist.

Clearly, "role of father", "role of mother", "role of parent" are all by declaration, by intentional act and are "created", not "found".

The only model which provides this clarity is the family model, to solve the puzzle, to provide the solution, to provide the evidence to clearly state: "created".

Summary:
Connection experience is created.

Chapter 6

The family model is the only "place" where this model is considered serious enough by enough serious people.

The "role of parent" is described in the book "The Visible Person: I" by a more inclusive word: category. Category includes "role", "group" and incredibly broader concepts. Category is debated outside of the family to such extremes that the possibility to even have a debate at all is of utmost concern.

Instead of attempting to include such debates about "found" or "created" about "category", about whether "rules for category" are "found" or "created", about whether every person ought to "just know" a "category exists" or that "rules for category exist" with complete expectation for ALL OF MANKIND to "just know" the "category" or "just know" the "rules" is NOT THE POINT.

The appropriate discussion is not about "know". The appropriate discussion is about "experience".

When "experience" is completely invisible, the discussion must include "where" the experience occurs. Although many have attempted to describe experiences "outside of the person", every experience actually occurs only "inside of the person". All experiences occur "inside of the person". This may cause concern by some and relief by others.

What becomes increasingly clear about experience, is Mankind depends completely upon experience to "know" anything. When "knowing" is attempted without experience, the attempt is always an unwitting failure. When "knowing" is claimed "knowable without experience", an unwitting failure is also experienced.

Knowing from experience is not certain knowing.

Knowing without experience is always certain knowing.

Knowing from experience is not certain knowing.

Knowing without experience is always certain knowing.

Only in the family, only by using "The Family Model", is this discussion possible. The use of "The Family Model" outside of the family is appropriate only by:

1. Acknowledge as foundational source "The Family Model" for all "knowing" by "category". This acknowledgment provides a means to discover or rediscover HOW the model ought to be applied.
2. Acknowledge as foundational source for "The Family Model" is TIP. This acknowledgment provides a means to include declaration-creates-perspective-experienced to enable an understanding for "experience required" to discover or rediscover HOW the experiencer of experience (TIP) is pre-requisite for all "knowing".

Summary:
The Family Model must be foundational for "The Category Model" implemented by Science, Law, Academia, Religion and Philosophy. (reference book "The Visible Person: I")

Chapter 7

Returning to Chapter 1 of this book: "rights within"

Any description or attempt to describe "rights within" as merely "found" and "known to be there" by whatever supporting reasoning may follow, is strange (perhaps insane) by one incredibly simple question:
Who claims to have actually experienced "rights within"?

When the person responding to the question makes presentation to support the "rights within" as "found" and known to be "within ____" (animal, rock, etc.), as though experience is unquestionably NOT part of the presentation at all.....then "Objection!" is appropriate. If "found" or discovered, who "found" these "rights within"? The presentation lacks appropriate support for "found" if no "witness" supports this supposed appropriate observation. Who provides actual testimony?

Observation of "rights within" requires an observer. Without an observer, how can an observation exist?

Only an observer having an actual experienced observation can claim or declare the observation important or valuable to "create the fact". Every observation is an experience. Every "fact" is an observation considered valuable enough to "share the claimed value". A claimed value is a declaration. Only a person (TIP) can actually make a declaration.

Summary:
"Rights within" cannot be "found".

Chapter 8

Declaration creates!

When the "observation" is created, it is the "observer" (TIP) who made the declaration. The declaration created the value which is sharable among Mankind. The declaration created the importance of the observation. The declaration created the possibility for connection by other members of Mankind through shared description of the observation, which is next considered by the listener as "category", which is next "category created within" that listener, which is followed by "connection experienced to category" by the listener.

After "category" is created by the listener, "rules for category" are shared by "observer" and listener considers the "rules for category" followed by declaration to create "rules for category" within followed by "connection experienced to rules for category" by the listener.

But the only "place" this description is taken serious by serious people is "The Family Model". The only "place" Mankind allows all of Mankind to accept this "create" possibility is in the family. The only place "category" (example: "role of parent"), "rules for category" (example: "rules for role of parent") and "connection" (examples: "connect to role of parent"; "connect to rules for role of parent") is in "The Family Model".

Only in the family model is "perspective" allowed to be a word with the much greater description, the superior meaning to "opinion". Only in the family model is distinction for "role of father", "role of mother" and "role of child" allowed to have such credibility as to "exist", to actually "be experienced" without "allowed debate".

When "The Family Model" is applied outside of the family, "experience" is not only attempted to be excluded, the appropriate description for the situation might be "forced" or "enforced" to be excluded. TIP might be described similarly excluded by "force" or "enforced" means.

But "The Family Model" remains inescapably and completely founded upon experience, and experience remains inescapably and completely founded upon TIP.

The depth, the details, the descriptions for what is "known" with such "clarity", with such "certainty" is subject to extremely simple foundational question:
- Who had the actual experience of the discovery?
- Who experienced the "rights within the cat"?
- Who experienced the "cause"?
- Who experienced the "connection"?
- Who experienced the "effect"?
- Who experienced the "group"?
- Who experienced the "role"?

When a response to the question is contention "for the question" as though the question is inappropriate, perhaps an appropriate question has been asked.

The objective herein is not to question IF an experience had actually been experienced. The objective herein is first to acknowledge that all knowing based upon "not experienced" is subject to causing problems for Mankind. The second objective herein is to acknowledge the source or foundation for knowledge is either BOTH "The Family Model" and TIP or just TIP.

Redirecting back to the beginning point in this chapter of this book: "rights within".

Mankind claims all members of Mankind have "rights within".

If this knowledge is not "found" to "be there" as though this is a type of "knowing" which every member of Mankind ought to just "know" as though self-evident, then what? And the simple question "Who experienced the rights within Mankind?" stirs unanswerable debate. And "found" also causes grave concern for unsolvable future debate that even a rock might "have" this same "rights within" some day. And no solution "reveals itself" to rescue Mankind from this clearly "certain knowledge" that an animal has "rights within"...... Perhaps Mankind must re-examine the process of "knowing".

Consider "The Family Model" the origin and foundation for this process of knowing. For "rights within" Mankind, consider Mankind is declared to have a right. Consider the origin of "right to continued life" to exist within Mankind originated by family, by parent. Consider "role of parent" gave authority to this person making declaration about offspring to "contain this right within". Consider "right within" is therefore created by declaration.

Likely, the "role of parent" might be considered again for "source of authority" to make that declaration that this "right within" exists. And then "source of authority" for that parent is likely to be considered again as "role of parent" is merely a "category" created by declaration which created a perspective which, when considered, will survive ANY amount of scrutiny to exist, and will also survive ANY amount of scrutiny as "experienced role of parent" and be foundationally unquestionably in "The Family Model". And this addresses "be there" appropriately as well (2 paragraphs above).

Then, to be thorough, declaration might be considered again for "source authority", whereupon TIP may be re-examined to exist (book "The Invisible Person"=TIP) to have any authority at all. And during that examination, the discovery will be that it is not TIP nor "experience" which UNQUESTIONABLY exists, is experienced and where "connection" is experienced, but the REAL discovery, the discovery of what is actually real, will be to discover TIP is entirely foundational and most real AND that what has been considered most real by so many serious people is "less real" than previously thought.

Summary:
The experience of "rights within" Mankind is a created experience by Mankind and the experience is appropriate and the creation act by Mankind is appropriate and the foundation for "rights within" Mankind is "The Family Model" and TIP.

www.ingramcontent.com/pod-product-compliance
Lightning Source LLC
Chambersburg PA
CBHW070134290526
45789CB00005B/2249